DEAD WHITE MALE

BRIAN
HERDMAN

**DEAD
WHITE
MALE**

DEAD WHITE MALE
A SHOALS OF STARLINGS PRESS BOOK
ISBN: 978-1-913767-24-2

Text copyright © Brian Herdman 2025
All artwork copyright © Andrew Martin 2025

The rights of Brian Herdman to be identified as the author of this work has been asserted by Shoals of Starlings Press

All rights are reserved. No part of this book may be used or reproduced in any matter whatsoever without written permission from the author, except in the case of brief quotations embodied in critical articles or reviews.

First published in 2025

Shoals of Starlings Press logo is copyright © Andrew Martin 2020

Shoals of Starlings Press is based in Plymouth, UK

Shoals
of Starlings Press

I too dislike it
— Marianne Moore

for Mouse

    I think of you.
    under a painted tree I lived in those days
    chaos in that space, even then, emerging
    yours though, was a dream room
    humming under your hand,
    the children leaping around you
    in shadow-play on the wall
    fair seed-time you gave them
    to wander the secret places, to echo down the years
    and sweet Jim there writing plays
    swathed in scarf and cigarette smoke
    posting those buff envelopes to the Royal Court
    how proud, how generous, how brave he was
    only those long years later to concede.
    and your holding-together of this
    nurtured all and nurtures yet,
    to live is to love, you were saying
    always kind, you knew the mystery,
    always did, always will,
    and though there's little enough of always left
    I find it's always still.

13 Dead white male
16 And if I chance to speak to someone far away
18 Cultural exchange
19 Impressionism
20 None of these organisms produce these reactions as a result of deliberation
21 Ivy
22 The ubiquity of biological complexity
23 According to Newton
24 A moment of gratitude
25 Fuimus fumis
26 Epistemology's a scam
27 Abstract impressionism
28 Autumn blues
29 Particle physics
30 How it happens
31 He must be dead now
32 Happiness is wiki
34 Politics
36 Succession
38 Her mental health
39 Thales
40 Is there a way out of this?
41 The answers perhaps
42 Time and the river and the mountain
43 History's a mess
44 There are no people
45 There is no soul
46 The state of things
47 I'm loving you now
48 Force majeure
49 Kandinsky: Lake Constance 1914
50 Dear sons
51 Swimming lessons
52 A postcard
53 Accidental birth
56 This smartwatch enhancing seniors' lives like never before
57 Coda to Psalm 130
58 Habit
59 Country blues
60 Dead zone
61 Box room

62	Old man
63	Ingenue
64	Plakias
65	Inside
66	I love you
68	Only once
69	Out on the sound
70	September 22nd 2020
72	See me
74	In green
75	Prepositions
76	Caught unawares
78	Marginalia
79	Three chords and the truth
80	Sorry I'm late
82	Topography
83	Unfamiliar territory
84	Soupcon
86	How come
88	Inside the yurt
90	Snow driven
91	North
92	A sadness
93	I'm listening to the Everly Brothers sing
94	Scorpion
95	Sexual intercourse
96	What we do, or don't
97	All the things that never happened
98	Chattel
100	Existentialism
101	Extreme unction
102	Ambulo ergo sum
104	Essential remains
107	In the garden
108	His life
110	End of life care
111	My dying breath
112	My life and other things that never happened
113	Fader
114	On reading Robert Herrick with the benefit of hindsight
115	Reading Peter Reading on the bus to the hospital

116	Reading Rilke on the bus to the hospital
117	Reading John Berryman on the bus to the hospital
118	If you are reading this, I am alive
120	The old place
123	Listen
124	All hope
125	Voices on a great sea rising and falling
126	Demise
127	How it happened
128	Post mortem
129	Squamous cell carcinoma
130	Elephant
133	There is a sickness at the heart of this
134	Song of living too long
136	Deadlines
138	Thinking about it
139	Absence
140	I've grown old
142	Redshift

Dead white male

I'm looking in the mirror, my face a front
north, north west 5

veering south, south west 2
losing its identity

skin is like history
its moves are slow

we all talk about it and
everybody has an opinion but

nobody knows what's going on
the time of day or why

it's always raining
and the light soaks deep

into the deep earth
where what we call god

lives indecipherable
as a murmur

the rumour of an equation
and all that lies behind us

of course, we mostly got it wrong
yet fault lies not here, but within

the heart's concordance of anguish
newsprint rots on the compost

of a future none knows nor can ever know;
the accumulated years, the cremated remains

of lives of waste of ruin and regret
of purpose intention and aims

a small boy weeping, a fairy tale
a broken toy, an angry exchange

I can see from here I'll be yours
one day to do with as you wish

I loved you once
but what loved is lost

blown over that border, that post,
one sees rows and rows of burning gas jets

and understands that
at a certain point romance

turns to tragedy
and if sperm is a dead end

the best strategy
is to do away with it, after all

what is remembered has been
saved from nothingness

and since the concentration camps
we have been exposed

to thousands of photographs
of the dying, of the dead

but nothing's that simple and
what you call law is mere reaction

you think you know what's going on
my friend you think you know

but the lights of the city bend
distort and peel away skin from our eyes

to sear imagination with the guilt
of ghosts that lie always with us

and no mere transition provides
a cure for that, it works both

ways my young friend and guilt
is the unerasable condition

the pornography of the soul
that forms and lies

like dirt on the snow it's
what remains of blood, what lingers

that filthy smell on our fingers
the ecstasy of our pain

for love is nothing more
than inability to be alone

I loved you once
but what loved is lost

when I say I, I mean we of course
and by we mean I confused

I loved you once
but what loved is lost

and what's loved is stilled
in stone and cold as an easterly

as you as me as all of us
cold, confused to receive

the mad confessor's benediction
in his box of ineluctable joys, the fruits of

ha'penny contritions, three hail marys
one our father and a glory be

let's leave it at that
let's wait and see

And if I chance to speak to someone far away

   for Mo Bottomley

a woman, a stranger, drunk,
smothered his face in wet kisses
leaned back to give him more regard
waved her forefinger, said, you

are a fraud. I said to him, interesting,
isn't it, what the drunk see,
have the courage to see,
see through us and it's true,

we are, all of us, frauds
how else could we live
without the masks we create,
the faces we present to others like us

afraid that
behind this bundle
of fleeting impressions
of a world we know nothing about,
we are at root,
nothing.

I am thinking alone here
looking out over the ocean
of the interminable nature
of our lives we know
but cannot fathom
will end

how silent the earth
save only the sea's relentless moan
how empty, vast and mysterious
it feels, how tense the sky
ballooning cloud
how painful to lose
the cruelties and sorrows
of this life

to which we cling
as to a raft in terror
on a swelling sea
and for what passing flotsam
of some happy chance.

Cultural exchange

that morning, outside my ground-floor flat
the morning of my first day
as I left to teach my first class
at 7.45 a.m. right there, in front of me,
a stocky man, white hat, oversized black suit
frayed and stained rust at the cuffs,
peasant hands, rough, ingrained with dirt
slit the throat of a cow tethered to a post
the animal buckled
fell slowly to ground
its three-hundred-degree long-suffering stare
rolled into mine, blank and uncomprehending
blood running dry into dry red dust
I had travelled far
and had much to learn.

Impressionism

your breath was hot on my neck
in the alcove by the Thames
that morning after the ferry back from France
where we waltzed round the water lilies
hungry for more.

thirty years later, we embraced again
in Taunton Dean services not knowing
we had been on the same bus from Heathrow
you recognised me though I am old now
still twenty years between us
I would never have recognised you
your youth fallen away
yet all the threads of a life
sewn in your grace as you moved
back to board the bus.

as we pulled into Plymouth
I gave you the Murakami I'd finished,
my number inside the back cover,
you gave me a square of your chocolate
that was you
I wished you well, then turned at the exit
to wave goodbye once more
the chocolate still sweet on my tongue.
and it's ok
that you didn't read the book.
it all fades without consequence
like the impressions
in that memory-foam mattress

None of these organisms produce these reactions as a result of deliberation

Antonio Damazio — Looking for Spinoza

the experience of time varies
it is time decides fate, where once
I had, so I believed, agency, now
all is hollow
all is hollow
all is
what remains within me
is what little
time I have left to reflect
and I am in no hurry
to get anywhere
in time or out

Ivy

> Fernando Pessoa — the play that goes on in transitional space
> is sometimes sexual in nature

in the sub
liminal self there is freedom
freedom to roam to pass
through pass out pass on
with an eye
in that one could in truth live
yet what kind of agreement there is
between thought and the great out-there
puzzles the sharpest minds
whilst every one of us should be capable of all ideas the
youngest among us reject the status quo and
the body's decline progresses like
the creep of ivy lost
to words over
a cemetery wall

The ubiquity of biological complexity

Marcus Chown — The Never-Ending Days of Being Dead

one hundred and eight thousand miles away
    from the very first words
what is the name of this double thing found
    at the seam of silence and speech
thoughtlessly fingering what cannot be grasped?
such sensation as we derive is derived
    only from the jokes we tell ourselves
on solitary nights when the still cold Spring air
drifts through windows left open for sleep
    my wife cries a little
and her tears falling through clouds reach
the stream of your tears that ends in the anxious hearts
    of men, her lovers, lost in darkness
for what purpose did you awaken within us
another day of nullity, vacuity, restlessness
and the impossibility of inert senseless matter?
in these rivers are
the source of all pain and worry

hope too, yet Freud once remarked
that the scientist has to work so hard
to achieve what the poet tosses off so easily.

According to Newton

no variation in things arises
from blind physical necessity
which must be the same always
and everywhere.
one begins with such certainties,
that the world is benign, that our parents
love us, that there is truth
out there waiting
to be found,
that all we need are the right tools
meanwhile
a child lies dead, face down, skin suppurating
on some foreign sand

and all the lies
gangsters and politicians peddle
and all the while
poets angle for metaphors to muddle
the waters
like so many illusive fish.

A moment of gratitude

he stood at the door and turned back around
looked at the clock on the wall
the crockery on hooks
one last time

the dark outside
in the shadows, beneath the trees
lying in wait

Fuimus fumis

we are smoke
we rise and drift and disappear
to haunt the spavined districts of our lives
the upended coffee tables of the cafes,
the dumb waiters, the abandoned shoes,
the tickets and torn photographs
of cities gutted in war
all those places, those sepia places,
burnt-out places and those never sought,
never gained, never lost,
never-coming-home-again places
anonymous, we drift with the wind that stirs
the litter through the follies and the fractures
and the silence in the shells
of lives unlived
undone by by circumstance
unlived, unloved, unkind.

Epistemology's a scam

y'know
whata y'know about whata y'know
and how long is a piece of string 'n
how far can y'make it str--etch,
or draw it out and leave no room for doubt
that it is in fact string yr talking about?

knowledge, like string and other things, ain't what
it used t'be since god quit and heaven's
forms eternal descended to minds
adrift in rhythms diurnal

spades back then were spades
and you could call them such
a rose was a rose truly a rose
and not by any other name known
nor some opening gambit

in modernist argument about what gives
and who gives what up.
what with Newton's quake
in Galileo's wake what a difference a day
can make to knowing
what's what and what's not.
confused? well, if not now,
you soon will be.

Abstract impressionism

like red
I is subjective substance
in objective shell

as art
I considers this and explores
limits which

are nothing
if not pliant if not
secure then not

Autumn blues

and the sky
collapsed
and wow!
a different road
the pavement
rose up
to climb
the hill
and meeting
the brow
white horses
on blue
rolling wide-angled away
on late
blue chill

Particle physics

we breathe in what we burn,
what we burn we breathe in,
what we breathe in,
is not air, is minute,
industrial, invisible,
ten million people each year die
worldwide from this.

as for me, I'm almost late,
helicopter blades,
like cut-ups, cut up
this heavy summer evening,
disturb the air I catch,
mine I catch,
mine I,
catch mine I,
catch.

How it happens

it was the kind of empty that fills
all the available space
he could hear

the mournful toll of
the Angelus bell from St John's
summoning the very Christ from the Word

imagined his wife bowing her head
in prayer over the dishes
or with the child at her breast, yes

she was a goodly soul and he had
chosen well, yet, with each stroke,
each step, came

another becquerel.

He must be dead now

it's cold and I'm walking down a cold street
I recall the time, remember how
I smelt his breath hot
down the phone line
heard him sweat down the phone
I-think-I-might-have-just-killed-someone
his breathing heavy
sweat seeping from the pustules
on his neck, on his face crimson
and yellow weeping sores, the eyes buried
in flesh thick as blubber, he wants
to keep me on I want to go
on not knowing
what to say, or caring in truth
what he has to say
save only for the dead man
waiting.

Happiness is wiki

I never want to hear from any cheerful Pollyannas
Who tell me fate supplies a mate
That's all bananas
sang Judy Garland in Girl Crazy

I am Janus, Ray Bradbury said,
both Pollyanna and Cassandra
warning of the future,
and living half-assed
ahead darkly
but rosy in the past

Hayley Mills in the film
of one of those names
played the Glad Game
pestering people all over town
like Pangloss of old
with sunshine and happy
and never being down

whereas Leibniz, who might be accused
unfair, or not,
of starting this rot

laid it all out in Monadology
God, he said, has the idea of infinitely many universes —
an idea which spiralled out of his control —
only one of these universes can actually exist —
to be taken up some 300 years later —
God has reason to choose one thing or another, —
by scientists who rejected the very idea of God —
is good, ergo, he said, with implacable logic —
and ran with it to the limits of the possible —
the universe that God chose to exist
makes for the best of all possible worlds.

but wait

it might be observed,
evil demands that
courage perfects
and the lie
signals the truth

more often than not
philosophical arguments clot
and philosophers
tie themselves up in knots

a mind can always conceive
of one more self-righteous Adam
for every wilful Eve.

Politics

out of our depth
not knowing where we are going, or how to get there.
there are those who would do us harm
those with insider signals
pitched above the common awareness or understanding
to keep us in ignorance, we poor,
systematically raped, pillaged and exploited by elites,
they keep us mute, we poor,
keep us poor,
pressed to the margins, we poor,
our lives constrained through wilful ignorance and want,
we lost,
we lost and poor.
our grievances run deep, deeper than the facts.
listen to our children, voices lost in the shudder of noise,
the fairy tales,
the policeman's knock, the social worker's call
saw nothing wrong, heard nothing untoward,
heard nothing at all, spoke
not a word for we poor
the Government Report
the shrieks of the forest
the wails of the long since dead
the machineries of the city
which beat against the very air we struggle to breathe.
When We Were Very Small,
we could not reach the table and scraps were thrown to the floor
for we poor, left guttering for stars are we poor
Now We Are Six
no one loves me, no one is going to feed me
a child's cries, caught on CCTV
in his parent's house alone, little Arthur Labinjo-Hughes,
soiled, bruised and weeping, sleeping
on the living room floor in his filth alone
such things —
even as the bruises colour them,
even as the carbon monoxide poisons them
even as they starve

even as the video captures them
subject to adult hands and worse —
such things as these,
turned into reports and reports into policy,
platitudes on slick political tongues
on rolling news-feeds and interviews on Newsnight
to keep the public ensured, ensnared in spin
it must never happen again, the dogs of privilege bark
in the House, or over dinner.
yet Ezras, Hamzas, Khyras, Stars, and Arthurs still cry,
no one loves us, no one is going to feed us,
this is allowed to happen
we are allowed to die.

Succession

I was thinking about what you said earlier
come to pay your respects
and with respect, I have to say,
I disagree. life after all
isn't like that, a funeral march, an
endless succession, one thing leading
inevitably to the other, a procession,
parades of triumph and glory, that's just

the way it feels sometimes when overwhelmed
by the triplicate symbols of power,
on cushioned purple display, the faithful
brought to heel through liturgical lies
or in-camera deals lap it up,
lap it all up, the imperatives to choose,
choose, or obey. think about it,

remove the specifics — the price of cheese
the gas and leccy bills, filthy air,
the disappearing ash, the oak and bonny rowan trees
and what's left is asthma and ambiguity
roadworks and congestion
corruption and condescension
and what you do about these
other than reach for and cling
to the wreckage of a past
surfing on irony, leaf-mould and radio-waves,

don't go there, don't go near
all you'll hear is mush, mush, mush
the white-noise of history's carnage
isn't history at all if you think
of those soldiers as toys.

now that it's all over, dressed up and ready
grim god save all happy and glorious
in towns and cities across the land
people gathered, gawping, vox popping

in mimic, harmonic servitude
I just had to come, said one
it's quite a big moment in history, another
she served the country magnificently, one more,
pulled the whole nation together
what will we do without her?
in this, they say, they believe

and those same soldiers in harnessed labour,
or with tippy-tappy steps, escort her,
slaves to the rhythm
of pipes, tub-thump 'n drum,
on that journey to her final resting place,
euphemisms polished, spruced up, still dumb
in English oak lined with lead
to keep her royal deadness
deader longer
than mere mortal dead.

Her mental health

she remembers rain and all that falls
read a book by Wilhelm Reich
but was unable to cure her appetite

Thales

he started it
the world is water, water is the world
that first Greek said
it was the kind of thing back then
flowed from old Greek heads
right or wrong,
and best keep an open mind, eh?
there's little doubt
of two worlds thus formed
we live in but one and
what we perceive is not
out there is not what is
but what's in here
is not the thing
as thing-in-itself
that's out there:
in here is
something else

Is there a way out of this?

what's going on?
who are all those people?
why are they here?
why are those cows lying down?
what do you mean, it's raining?
what is?
why do birds suddenly appear every time you are near?
are you sure this is the right way?
what is the right way?
why do things always have to change?
what's the point of putting a sign there?
why is he always shouting?
why doesn't he pipe down?
why is she so quiet?
why doesn't she speak up?
what's the matter with them?
what else can you do?
is that it?
do you know the way to San Jose?
well, what's the point of anything?
where do you get off?
what's the matter with you?
is that all?
have you got any more?
why do you bother?
where are you going with this?
can you see a pattern here?
why do you ask?
what exactly do you want to know?

The answers perhaps

lie herein
nobody knows
they are just the people
milling about in the rain
it's raining, always raining
the sky it is heavy and dark
they sing to remind themselves
and you
of another day and all the other days
no one can ever be sure
directions — assays in blind space
continuity — an illusion
there perhaps to indicate there is life yet
in order to assert over the silence
he has lost the art
she knows her place and favours
peace despite the bruises
you do what you can and no more
everybody knows that old tune
there is no point
this next stop is mine
yours the one after
as clear as day when you open your eyes
because I need answers
because I need to know
if I knew I wouldn't be asking

Time and the river and the mountain

these are our permanencies
we shall speak no more of our heroes
now that they are dead, or speak only the truth
what are you, stranger, smeared in blood
slap-slithering like trout in her hand?
what brings you here? what fault deferred
defines your law, engineers your reason?
these events, we must conclude, are superficial
manifestations of rumours in the substrate.
politicians, said Cicero, are not born
they are excreted.

History's a mess

it all hangs from hooks

we've never been close
a sky distressed

and now, proscribed
our lives are less

how did we get here?
you ask

and more opinion
collapsed into books.

There are no people

no stars no sky
                              torn away
no eyes to see
                              hope is not

                              some crazed idea

There is no soul

only words
                        we use
to make
us
                    what
                  we
feel
we   are
are
        not

The state of things

back in the day
when things were neither large or small
everything clear as Greek light
the sun, the moon, planets and stars
an eternal backdrop to a drama
conceived, cast, directed and watched over
by God, what we did
or did not
do
mattered
to the way things were, was, in God's truth
what the way-things-were was put there for
in the first place.
then along came Copernicus
and other upstarts and it turned out
that things weren't exactly the way
they were previously and that the universe
was a whole lot bigger
than previously thought, that
the earth and the world were no longer
interchangeable terms, that the one
was phenomena, the other idea
                 and open
to all manner of interpretation and that we
were no longer at the centre of the drama
as it played out
that perhaps there was no centre at all
and no drama
that maybe it just goes on and on and on
expanding in all directions outward
and God only knows what happened to God
who somehow got lost in all of this
confusion and lack of certainty
about where exactly we stood in relation
to it all, let alone
to each other.

I'm loving you now

as I never did before
because when I loved you then
I could not love you more
not knowing you or who I was
knowing then as I do now
it was all too much
solid as I was
caged
now hollowed out
it all dawns on me

Force majeure

reality is a simulation subliminal

don't kid yourself, kid, every day's a front
for the mastications of parasites
and machinations of alien forces
which possess, control and have designs on us

what was irredeemably malevolent about the Nazis
was their willingness to submit and die for the cause

when Zhuangzi awoke, he realised he couldn't be sure
if he dreamed of being a butterfly
or if the butterfly dreamed of being Zhuangzi

wait'll you see, Annie my love,
we'll build castles from our dreams
so we will

things were worse than he imagined
much worse than he imagined
reached deep and
deeper into the cold ground
and were not easily shifted
but what cannot be owned
cannot be stolen

the war began at 11 a.m.

Kandinsky: Lake Constance 1914

desist listen
a butterfly ripple
from thought to thought

to the thought of thought
flags pull at the wind flap crack
snap back

steel links clink against the flag-poles
as he drinks the harbour lights
blink from blue to red to blue

each wing trembling on the brink
of expression
draws the storm

Dear sons

everything's fine over here
an amazing place,
not a thought in the sky
listen, still finding my feet
god knows where they are
I don't have much time
they're not big on time here
but just wanted to say,
it all passed without much fuss
sweet as a nut
didn't feel a thing
no pain at all
think I even left a smile behind
in the room — some long faces there
I can tell you, Jesus,
they need to get over themselves!
anyway, suddenly bright, it began again
without me, only the fading antiseptic
sense of me lingers.
one thing I don't get,
if this is the result,
all that stuff that came before,
all those years, all those words —
what were they all about?
step lightly
Dad

Swimming lessons

all the talk on TV this hot afternoon
is of loss and war and dying too soon
a door slams shut to destroy Sunday's grace
the aircon trembles through the window's lace
its shadows dance like truths upon the wall
the heat stifles, life stops but you feel it all

the same, its hand heavy, inert, dense as lead
the sky a fierce blue, the sun blinds
slathered in sunscreen, splashing about in the pool
they learn to swim, that to drown's not an option
anyone accepts any more than they accept
that you just don't like cabbage, cold
shoved to the side of the plate in tears
learn in the real world choice is elided
and the dead, away from Mario Kart,
are ever-present, ever-lost, ever-needed.

A postcard

picture this
a man sits
at a bar
in the sun
drunk drinking
wistful in
Myrthios
Crete staring
out to sea
It's high noon
been drinking
since nine or
thereabouts
three hours drunk
he'll keep on
drunk drinking
whatever
comes his way
for the next
twenty years
understands
nothing and
underneath
his skin he
is at war
with himself
emotion
sluices up
like crude oil
on the waves
of his fear
and at night
in his ear

Accidental birth

and maybe you're out walking one day
and wondering what makes a poem,
and maybe you think, it's like this,
like you might be seventeen, or eighteen years old
and sat in one of those downtown arthouse cinemas
the Cinephone on Market Street, or the BFI Oxford Road
and maybe you've smoked a little blow beforehand
and you're watching the show
when something shifts...

I dunno, a jumpcut was it, or some latecomer,
and your mind starts to drift somewhere out of there,
that specific place, to some other place, smokier, less defined
and you find yourself thinking sudden
of Jean-Luc Goddard being dead
and even though said event is many years
and a million motion pictures from now, you know,
don't question how you know, just know it, know
he changed the whole direction of that tracking-shot
the way it was going, right there, right then
and it's not even his film they're showing, when

something else shifts, someone eating a hotdog
or maybe some nuts,
and you are back at the screen
and you know, with the certainty of a razor cut,
you know this is a moment,
a split second's all it takes
to get out your pen and notebook in the dark
and write down the words that come from the screen
as you hear them
and your mind jumps back and forth
to what's just been said and what's being said
and you get the gist and know that this
this seeming... this inconsequential scene —

a man alone in his car, overlooking this city
somewhere out there on the west coast of

the united states of america —
know that moment,
that scene, those words, pouring from that screen
are crucial to who you are now and who you will be
those long years ahead when Jean-Luc Goddard is dead
and the queen is dead and your father so long dead
and your brother dead and your mother is dead
and your wife and there's a wound
inside that will never heal
and all the leaves fallen from all the trees, all dead,
all dead all around you, and the dying all around you
and you carry them with you further
and that scene imprinted in your head
and the words in the dark with paper and pen in your head
and all of it takes you to the world of the poets and miscreants
the musicians and mutants and the lost tribes of Israel
gathered there, Asher, Dan, Ephraim, Gad
Issachar, Manasseh, Naphtali, Reuben
and the two other tribes of Judah and Benjamin,
and the Phoenicians were there, the Philistines,
Egyptians and artists of all descriptions were there.

or, it's the young man, to this town lately come,
a young man of the streets, a homeless man, maybe,
who hovers behind as you write these words

and I think

he wants money, but no,
he just wants to show me, and ask me about this dragonfly
he's found lying on the road and now holds
in the palm of his hand to show and say, what should I do
with this little fella, man, its body like a spool of silver foil
unfurled on his palm and its wings spread wide catching
iridescent the light of the sun, and I say, Ah, man!

just let him go, he'll be fine, let him fly,
they live, I said, only one day, and then die.
and he says, Oh! I didn't know that,
and the wings on his palm tremble a touch,

I didn't know,
and his voice trembles a touch
and I say, yeah, that's how it is.
I'll put him down
here, he says, on this leaf, gentle as gentle is,
mind how you go, man, he says, before he leaves.
you too, man, you too, I say, take care,
that's just how it is, don't worry, let it come,
let it all come to you
it's alright, that's just how it is.
and maybe it's this has made a poem.

and all of, and in between all of, the shit
that pours into and out of your head you know
this scene, this moment now,
you somehow have to get behind it,
this time, this place, these words, this screen and write it,
write the words, write it all down, how it is,
how it exists, how it all survives, how it dies
how it is, or is not born,
is beyond even that potentiality
and know, know this moment
a poem somewhere exists because of words written
on a page, in a book, in the dark, a lifetime ago.

This smartwatch enhancing seniors' lives like never before

in a deep state, in abstraction,
in extremis is the simulation
of clarity in the moment
before death is time
collapsing is poetry
is hope in action
that final exhalation
that annihilation of despair
is ah!
is all revealed
is as nothing
is all poetry,
is all art,
all music is
death is nothing
is time revealed
is time as no-time
is nothing before it began
is nothing

continues as nothing

is absence is all
is some thing
out of no thing
is all of nothing
is all there
is is
is being language
is language
is it

Coda to Psalm 130

    after e e cummings
        for Jen Hawkings, Abbie, Alistair and Lauren,
        for the loan of the house

to be
to be in a house
to be in a house with children
their laughter uproarious
around the breakfast table
to be
to be in a house
to be in a house of light
and laughter uproarious
when it's Spring
in Just
Spring after dark
and laughter and light springs
forth after dark and Spring's
delicious after dark
light
to be
to be in a house
of light and laughter
sprung, de profundis
stepping lightly
in true Spring. Oh
(!) this Delightful
and /
or this daffodil

Habit

Father O'Connor, sipping the saccharin
beneath his tongue, his breath hot
in the box, sweat beading his brow, Breviary
to hand and fingers entwined in the knots
of his Rosary contemplates
The Sorrowful Mysteries of Christ
this being Tuesday, a slow day
in the confessional, he wishes he had brought
The Sporting Life but waits patiently for the virgin
on the other side of the screen to speak, clears
his throat and breathes in his living.

Country blues

   for Becca Langsford

I'm listening to Gillian Welch
she's been in the Lowlands
way too long, sings

make me down a pallet on your floor
and phrases the vowels to plead
make me down a pallet soft and low
babe I'm broken and I got nowhere to go

and I think of Becca
of how she sang — sings — these lines
of how long it is since I heard
that tear-stained voice
that lifts us high and draws us close
that wets its finger for seeds
broadcast on a southern breeze
and channels the signals
of Minnie and Bessie and Billie
to slide and sleaze through
booze and boudoirs, boxcars and bars
far away from here
up town Chicago
out of our time, out of town
timeless in time now
on a fast train or slow
out of our reach and bring it all
keening back home
on a transatlantic call.

Dead zone

thing is
I'm out drinking in The Dolphin
a companion either side of me
Phil who's blind and doesn't know
what's going on around him anymore
and another guy who's barking in my ear
and all of it about him, his life, his opinions
the usual shit, the wife, the kids, those long years
since whenever it was, makes y'proud, he's saying,
loud enough for the rest of the pub to hear,
like I should be interested, like they should
and out of the corner of my eye
I catch Phil swallow-diving into
one of those delirious monologues
that beset him in drink when left alone
about how to fix the world, something
he's heard on radio 4 and snapping
his fingers, his head nodding and bobbing back
and forward, and side to side at no-one
in particular on this side of the bar
or behind it, occasionally chuckling
at something he's said to himself
he turned seventy this week but was on
antibiotics at the time so it's
only now we are having a
celebratory drink, buying time

Jesus!

I'm nowhere near
where I thought I'd be,
it's nearly six,
I think

Box room

I'm sitting here in this square box of a room
with a low, low ceiling and lack of natural light
I have to keep the damned electricity on all the time
and all the time I'm sitting here thinking
about the way things are and the way
I'd like them to be when

I am struck by a thought that all the stuff
I think I own, all the detritus of my days on earth,
that I drag around from place to place from pillar
to post, so to speak —

post being the operative word
here as I draw ever closer to my non-existence,
my subsequence, which is itself a form of existence now
in the minds of people who knew me, a possession
of sorts of this entity, me, which in their minds
becomes him, or he, or even you if they're getting intimate
with the thought of me or raising the subject
with others, my children, say, or grandchildren
or friends, or drinking companions, who might hear
a tune on the jukebox maybe and say he,
he would have loved this, that's his kinda tune
and think about me for a moment before passing
on to the next event that happens
across their horizon
leaving me unable to either confirm or deny
their observation —

all this stuff, that just happens to have found its
way into my locality and to which I lay claim
so much so that sometimes I offer to loan it out
as in, would you like to borrow it?
or, please, take my seat, your need
is greater than mine,
and anyway, I need to stretch my legs:
all this stuff is in truth
simply the matter of time.

Old man

I imagine us down the pub
a few pints, watching the footy, khaki forgotten.
red or blue, it's up to you, your choice:
hold us together, or further divide
as you take one side or the other.
or would that brute, lately come back, adapt
and smack it into the back of the net?
futures are nothing if not driven
as traffic flow stalls, directions are lost —
what's a past but a future broken?

Ingenue

I love him now, that youth, not so much then,
though in truth I barely knew him at all
his awkward insouciance, trying to carry off
that brown needlecord jacket, a touch too large
over his slender frame, that deep blue shirt
open-necked, natty, or so he thought.

his beautiful face, smooth alabaster
not yet cut by years, his light brown hair
kiss-curling over the ears and those eyes
deep, lost blue in shadow, no wonder
they were falling over themselves.

not that he knew, those hands attentive
as silk on skin, searching without
for what could only be found within.
I love him now, that youth, if only
he could have loved me then, that ingenue

standing on the Hungerford footbridge
linking Waterloo and Charing Cross
Blond On Blond and books stolen
from Foyles in his bag
The Spirit of the Age, Ionesco

comically absurd, careless even,
trains rattled past, he felt the structure shake,
looked over his shoulder, but, in breathing,
never saw it coming
nor which way it then went

Plakias

I know this place
blue Libyan sea before me
and mountains rising behind
I sink into
an ordinary day
all of forty years ago
smoking marijuana on the beach
with the German guy and his sister
cropped blond her hair
mine henna-red and wild
her young breasts still
the trivia and minutiae
of the conversation
ranging through the morning
to the meltemi raising sand
the colours and the light
how important it all seemed
to fix, to impress, to hold
the blue in mind the olives
green and whistling
that night climbing home
to the taverna
drenched in blues and golds and greens
such desire
        unslaked
and holding it
all those mornings since
and here in this cement box
        dispensing it

Inside

here it's quiet
only breathing escapes to the great
outside everywhere
not even the sound of the dehumidifier
sucking dry the air
disturbs my joy in time

that it is short but long enough
when I consider how little
I cared for this form how little

I gave shape to its cries
preferring instead to
take the next breath

I love you

please be seated
what in actual fact do we own?
our remarks, perhaps?
the parts of ourselves, perhaps,
not yet discovered?
comes a time when all you must decide
is which hat
everything else is done.
I make this stuff up
the bills are paid
I make it up and lean back into the wind,
notice when passing the news stand,
headlines about new cures for dementia
remember to take the pills and hope
to squeeze another five years
out of this all too sullied flesh.

cold memories
like blood coagulated, seal a child's tears
pooling on your palm,
the sound of sirens in another street,
the runaway train came down the hill and she blew,
voices in another room,
Al Jolson on the gramophone,
Listen With Mother, Journey Into Space,

the squeak of your ironing board,
rain pelting the window,
Jesus, Mary and Joseph, you cried,
will it never cease!

it's a stretch but feel it
there's no time like now
a darkness in which to drift delirious
nearer than now
nearer than touch
far away.

oh yes, darlin' I'd pick you up
and swing you wild again outside the
Jeu de Paume, giddy on the edge
over the traffic roar of the street,
the concerted blast of the horns,
of the city below
your laughter there and all that's lost
and about to become.

Only once

most everything else is shit
there's little here to stir the blood
the surfaces wiped clean, sparkle
hard granite shapes lives proscribed
by TV schedules and lousy food
meat on meat, shrink-wrapped and cheap

they don't believe the evidence.

Marx was of course wrong
nothing is determined
except misery.

she blames it all
on them bloody foreigners.
he says nowt.

Out on the sound

    for Molly Erin McCarthy, artist

a frigate anchored
three yachts, a gull skims the waves
enriched with ozone, fried fish and chips
diesel exhaust from the ice cream vans
comingled with the sweet
rich smell of
skunk
the world is always there
I wouldn't change a thing
the world is always changing
the world it shines
I wouldn't change a thing
the world is always shining.
I wouldn't change a thing
the patter from the mic on the tourist boat
a trail bike farts past on Grand Parade
from a red car Cliff and the Shadows
move it along the breeze
the sea licking breeze licking sea
this moment
all this and me?
I wouldn't change a thing

September 22nd 2020

for Andrew Martin

one day you wake up and discover that the future has found you
that change is behind you, that things will remain the same
that it's always been this way
that the changes you made in your head in the past
when you were careering towards something
a career maybe
or a family with a house and furniture and all,
that book you were gonna write,
or the other one
a winning lottery ticket
all the stuff out there waiting for you, all of that stuff
has gone
like it was never there in the first place —
it was never there in the first place —
think of that
think of what that means
and all the stuff that remains
and all the stuff that never happened
and all the stuff that did
and all the fucking books on all the fucking shelves
you bought thinking you were buying the fucking time
to read them all
only that illusion persists and well maybe
one day
one day you won't give up
and you'll pick up where you left off
one day
forget to eat and turn the pages
keep turning the pages of Infinite Jest
one day
call a friend who maybe feels the same
as you and say,
let's leave this shit behind,
let's do something different today
make an early start
head off somewhere find some clean air

find something in this
something to celebrate in this
the life of a poet maybe
yeah, I know, all the good ones are dead
but as of this day
Lawrence Ferlinghetti's still alive
let's celebrate that
like now, before it's too late

See me

see me, I got a dog
got it in the first lockdown
it's a lockdown dog
not a real dog
it's an in-my-mind dog
an in-my-mind lop-eared lolloping dog
got a band too
I call it The Lockdown Dogs
after my dog
and, like my dog,
it's not a real band
it's an in-my-mind band
an in-my-mind racket-creating band
and my dog is the kind of dog
I'd like to have in real life if I got a dog
it's a life-size dog
and chases pigeons
without ever catching them
until giving up confused
and bewildered by the whole enterprise
of being a dog owned by me,
acquired in lockdown,
confused by its role,
what it's supposed to do,
to be like, being a dog, my dog,
a lockdown dog
and my band, The Lockdown Dogs,
like my dog
being the kind of band I'd have
if I was in a band, plays the kind of music
that's not the kind that wafts
through the curtains of suburban households
on summer-hot afternoons,
but the kind of music I like to hear
in my head when I'm out walking
and thinking about all the dogs
I never had to walk.
and all the bands I was never in

and not the kind of bands I've been in
which never measured up to,
and in fact, fell someway short of
the kind of in-my-mind band
I hear when I think about bands
and were, those real bands,
like the dog
I'd have ended up with
if I had got a real dog,
barking,
recalcitrant, irascible,
refusing to heel and always, always
shitting in inappropriate places,
the kind of dog that stinks of life
as I live it
and the kind of band that sounds like the world
as I hear it

In green

took my dog for a walk
when halfway there
I realised

I don't have a dog
so I turned around
and took her back again

Prepositions

this is where, when we found ourselves
lost in play,
the Corona man trundled up with stone flagons of pop
the ragbone man inflated balloons for old clothes
the gypsy women selling clothes-pegs, shoelaces and fortunes
knocked for pennies or a curse
the blood in the sawdust on the butcher's floor,
the sip-sip of the bacon slicer
the greaseproof on the co-op shelf downstairs
and the foghorns pulsing low over Belfast roofs
up high in the dark wood bedroom
reading Sherlock Holmes after dark
in the dark-wood bedroom, searching.

dog paws dog walking dog grooming

all there, all parked up they stare
out to sea through windscreens
too much time to stop
they stare into the screens
of devices no
         diving
         no
         tomb-stoning
         danger of death
they scrawl
annual wall rocket
diplotaxis muralis
lovely yellow flowers
SCRAG says
the gospel according to Jack
is first thought best thought

the past erupts
bubbles up through the cracks
in the pavement and the wall

if you have problems pray
Jesus is with you, Jesus is ok

Caught unawares

my place or your place
it makes a difference
I love these shoes, so light
I bounce along in them they
take me anywhere I want to go
maximum ambulatory pleasure
why only today, following a fruitful trip to Lidl,
I was taken to drinking in the sun in Auntie's back yard
how far we have come, I said to him, or perhaps
just thought because sometimes the one never
becomes the other and it's that which is unsaid
impregnates and informs the moments that pass by
the moments that pass by the moments that pass
inflating the mystery of things, the disorder of the past.
Auntie spoke of Luddites of saxophones and singers
and OJ called, cycled back from Torpoint
I said I'd ring him later but never did
tired after dinner and sometimes,
sometimes
it just seems wrong
to prolong the event
better to let it slide, let things slide
it will go on anyway, things go on
things go on and things go on, that's
how it is
and I extend my territory from my place —

two cubic rooms facing north no sun, no light
no pets, just as well you couldn't swing a cat,
where my neighbours, all facing oblivion,
gossiping in the garden and
avoiding the bleeding obvious,
tend to the weeds —

from my place, then,
to outer space
alerted by the blackbird I exit and tramp

over the footbridge past the aquarium
through Teats Hill and Queen Anne's Battery
up Breakwater Hill looping round Cattedown Road
plumbing, heating, drainage
systems splitting space and time and weather
and the long memories of Sunday afternoons
all woven together
when we were young, love
and you were alive, love
with the spirit inside you, love
and the kids running their rings around us
in the bar of the Breakwater
dancing to Watershed
Noise Annoys, Two Bones and a Pick
The Black Buddha Band
the Works or The Bricks
and Your Local Oil Supplier skinning up in the alley
and that crazy rabble in beads and bangles
oil, leather, motorbikes and sandals

or the time we sat, you and I,
with the PEACE sign, anarchic red and black,
on the Hoe
below the war memorial, fasting
that long summer week for Peace,
for the peace we never found,

you never found until
the thing growing inside
years later
took your breath away

Marginalia

poets work in the margins, they lead hungry lives
whereas I'm fulfilled
and need only to hear the ocean
at summer's height wash against the rocks to know,

every time we say goodbye, I die a little.

or a tree alive with sparrows at dawn to know,
maybe today's a good day to buy a lottery ticket
because it's time and how we deal with it
is the measure of us.

suppose someone happened to observe
your movements now
how would you explain yourself?

what exactly are you doing?

Three chords and the truth

It's that time
just before the light fails
and things are fading away
and it just happens to be John Prine
singing about the peaceful waters
of Lake Marie
John Prine his body scarred
and scabbed over by the cancers
splits showing
opening into fissures where the light
floods out and it's
how the lyric curls
like the smoke from his Camels
drifting through the scenes in a projection beam
in a Saturday evening cinema
a long time ago before remembering
before knowing that you were remembering
that regular round of chords in key of G
like they are all he knows
like the only other song he has ever heard
is Madam George and has taken it
to his great expansive and
transcendent heart
or maybe it's Rainy Night In Soho
takes you to some other
same place
Shane slurring his words
toothless through
years of abusive
nicotine booze and smack
after all that damage
the light escaping
through the cracks
as song
or is it another light
comes shining
from the west
down
to the east?

Sorry I'm late

I'm listening to Gillian Welch
oh me oh my oh
she's singing of Miss Ohio who's
running around with her rag-top down
and, like Augustine, wants to do right
but not right now
and I'm thinking of my years
and how when my hair tumbled
royal over my shoulders
and me careening barefoot around these streets
frivolous, unhinged from care
or considerations of tense
no mobiles back then, no beeps or bleeps,
no boomboxes to disturb the peace
and only the distant traffic sending
quivers through the air eternal
the sea then was the sea
is still the sea and the sky
like an eye open wide in amazement
and limitless
blinked to kiss
the imagined blue line
beyond which lay history
and not the distraction on my wrist
at which I glanced one last time
then ripped off to give
to the bemused stranger
male, of middle years, passing by
on North Hill:
it means nothing, man, I said
glancing back, neither time nor
that second-hand Omega my parents had given me
they're long gone now and I wonder
does that watch still tick on his wrist
or another's, each second the same
as the one before and the one after
and each life lived the same
as the one before and the one after
must end

oh, the girls were pretty then
though prettier by far
now they are no longer mine

back then I was looking for good places to trip
now I keep finding places to fall
it means nothing, I said then,
now I find it means all.

Topography

    for Hans Olsson who never did send the socks

the lights of Bremen burn my skin
yellow my face
pressed to the window
rain falls slant
the bus is sleeping the engine thrums,
night bores on breathing heavy
and smooth as the cognac bottle
I use to nurse my guilt
on my way from somewhere
to somewhere else
for someone else to press flesh with
that it should fall, all fall away
that it should fall
all fall
to this road
this city
these lights,
the lights of Bremen,
yellow sparking scintillas
spray from wheels,
illuminate stray pedestrians on their way home
lost — their faces cryptic as ciphers,
shrouded like disgraced clerics —
they press towards doorways
exits and the sheltering dark without

Unfamiliar territory

It's all over for them.
I move from room to room
sniffing them out
wary, like a cat, as she busies herself
with dishes and rags and roses
her face soured by the years
and himself slumped in front of his screens

the silence curls like smoke between us

a silence punctured only by exclamations
oh, he might grunt as he shifts on the couch
oh, just the usual, cleaning, she responds
to a question about what the day might hold.
that weary slope of the shoulder
that dip of the head
as she stalks the kitchen
a pigeon
pecking at crumbs.

Soupcon

they were what — nineteen or twenty? —
and sitting cross-legged on the pavement
outside the Skiving Skolar, smoking adult cigarettes,
these two girls, students, I guess, and deep into
the kind of serious conversation
that only the young can have,
and as I approached them,
on my way home from an early evening gig
in the Fortescue to celebrate Nikki's birthday,
a bunch of us there, listening to our friend Rob C,
his guitar and singing rising above the convivial hubbub
and laughing, laughing long and loud
with my companions over — amongst all the other nonsense
we laugh about when out drinking with friends —
the ultimate recipe for leek and potato soup.
I was of the opinion that my favoured addition of a carrot —
sliced and cut into half moons to add a dash of colour —
did not constitute a violation,
but was rather, a variation of the classic recipe,
a new reading, if you like, an individual flourish
which offered up subtle new tastes, hints
to enhance, rather than, as my companions insisted,
completely departing from leek and potato to become
simply, vegetable soup,
and as I passed the girls, thinking about this,
thinking about friends and music and drinking and laughter
and our time here which is short
and getting shorter,
one said to the other,
looking down the long, foggy road ahead,

You know life, is not so bad,

and I, nearly sixty years their senior and looking back
down that same long dusty road at them,
smiled
and thought, they're not wrong, they're not wrong!
despite all the shit we wade through every day,

despite the news,
despite the war 'n the waste 'n the weather
life's not so bad, the kids are right,
the kids are all right, it's not so bad,
we can get through this

How come

you found yourself in the world
and the world in you
cried
that you should wake up
one morning and stride out
with blind purpose
seeking that of which
you know nothing
except that you must know
that you should travel
two thousand miles
to a beach
to drink cold beer and retsina
and stray fingers
happen across
the tiny stone Buddha
on the beach
a beach from which
a mountain rose
that you should fall drunk
on your back
on the road
as you climbed
that mountain
that night
that the stars
should rush down
on your fear
on your misery
that the truck
whose headlights you mistook
in drunkenness
for an ethereal
event whose
horn caused you
to scramble aside
pick up your
bits and pieces

not forgetting
the tiny Buddha
and stagger on
alive
past creaking
olive groves
until the bouzouki
and red light
of the taverna
announced that
it was not too late
that there was
time yet
to fill
time yet
to change

Inside the yurt

on the Tibetan plateau
we had been eating
crudely butchered and boiled mutton
with our fingers and garlic to rub.
she approached me singing
offering a bowl of baijiu
80% proof
you must drink as she sings
my host had said
for as long as she sings
you must drink
in the spirit of cultural harmony
I obliged.
her voice rose and fell in waves
as she sang
of the sorrows of a tribe
of the wind in the grass
and the yaks outside
the tintinnabulation of the bells
as she sang and I drank
the wind rose and the yurt
strained at the ropes
and my eyes strained and rolled
round as I drank as she sang
the room blurred her cheeks blooming red
there were knives,
I remember they were singing
as I drank as she sang
my host's teeth yellowing
and laughter mocking,
goading or encouraging
it's hard now to tell
as she sang as I drank as I wavered

oh, the plateau was wide, so wide,
miles wide and miles long

as I drank as she sang
of history's horizons
the spirit inside gave way,
and I passed.
the stench of mutton remains
is all next day I remembered
wild garlic on my tongue.

Snow driven

it could be a dream
the repeated thought of someone
already dead how it begins
how it ends with snow
begins with snow and thoughts drifting
like flakes of snow
drifting through a cold night's
driving through snow
dead thoughts
thoughts absolved
of corporeality
that refuse to fade
he hears them though
they are not his thoughts
can taste them like snow
flakes on the tongue
and the insurgent swipe
of the wipers wipe
out each to
each fro
each thought
each dead
each begin

North

mine is a northern voice
modulated under northern skies
of parents from the north of Ireland
northern vowels
rolled like the Pennines
on the western side
you could hear the thunder
rumble across a city black and bloodied from war
dragging my mother's impoverished tears
and roll away to those hills to bounce
back again with a second wave.

her hands red raw rise dripping
foaming from the sink
to scrub my knees with a flannel
stinging as they dry, I sit wailing
on the draining board, watch rivulets
of rain chase each other
down the window pane and the hills
those hills across the rhubarb fields.
like dark clouds so far away.

A sadness

it was wallpaper, or maybe snow,
a dream of snow falling as in the ending
of The Dead, so slow,
still almost, as if God had materialised
and declared, it shall be
cold and still

as death and everyone you've known
taken by a sadness, there is
a sadness befalls them, bent,
leaning in to the still wind,
trudging through snow
cold and still.

I'm listening to the Everly Brothers sing

bye bye love and staring at the painting
you made of psychotic trees, love
covering the lacuna between books on my shelf
is this really you, love?

asking
for a friend
who's looking
for answers of his own, a
friend of his own, this friend, love,
whose roots rummage deep and wide yet
show so little above it's hard to understand how
the music that trembles in his fingers like autumnal
leaves about to fall to dance
over the strings seems so — effortless

or how the mandolin lines
creasing his brow seem so at odds
with what it is like to hear
love fracturing the face
when about to tip from inner
to outer space

Scorpion

I saw it once long ago
you were more beautiful than death
and carried sky and earth within
the smog-heat of Athens traffic in July
all washed away and forgiven
your story erased
your fault-lines smudged
you grew a carapace
a smile slipped inside shadow
an exoskeleton hugging walls
perimeters, the edges of things
you assumed the dust of corners
gone dry, friendless, infertile
to ground shifting
with spiders and mites.

now your blood's beating is near,
is with that same earth,
that same sky turned crimson

the sun long down
I embrace the light that remains

Sexual intercourse

that afternoon on the hotel roof
everyone else had fled to the beach
we found ourselves alone
heat sucked sweat from our skin
as we fucked ourselves desperate
breathless apart.

What we do, or don't

one thing to be said for this tomfoolery
is that it displays a degree
of optimism and makes my heart
sing despite — or maybe because of —
the stent therein deployed
and the many other ailments
which ravage my unloved body.

All the things that never happened

happened to us that day in June
whose lives sleep with yours
in the heat now
and on the day
you were born
and every day since
and every cut you made
every trip, each stumble
all laughter, all tears
all of thirty-five years
all of and only.

Chattel

time to take off your clothes love
morphine's sentinel by your side will ease the flow
the air is green now your breathing slower slows
your sister-moth-bird-bat rattling the window
trying to get in on your act.

time to take off your clothes love
you are now entering marginalia.

time to take off your clothes love
your boys alive now and grown —
we are all of us grown — hold you still
and tread the fine lines sown between us
they're all that's left of us love
the best of us love and carry the seeds
of the unimaginable impossibility of being dead
my love and what's left love
the voices of children playing in the park
the great sea out there emblazoned by the sun
the wink of a wifi eye in the dark
such rude awakenings such bitter pills to swallow
such obscenities as these and others to follow
we were always better than this.

take off your clothes love
leave them behind, one step in the dark, just one step
look at it this way empty days run into empty days
nights aghast with sorrow spawn diseased fruit
and breathe in peculiar ways
how it is now how it has been how it will be
I'm not unhappy everything turns
some cycles are long some heavy
some we measure some never.

time to take off your clothes love
remember the house we built from scratch
bottom to top

the spider plants geraniums and yucca
the sweet smell of loam
mist that lingers on morning lanes
the chatter of rooks we talked of things
of kitchens and bedrooms canvas and books
the captain's chair riddled with worm
we had always with us.

Existentialism

look
there's nothing for you here
why hang around
I understand you are not as quick
on your feet, or the uptake
as you used to be. I'm told you don't
spit or rattle as you used to
a damp squib you might say
and no
I am not trying to tell you
what you should do
just that I think it's
about time, it's always
about time
and if I were in your shoes —
no, I know I'm not
but if I were —
well,
you've never been one
to shy away
from taking a plunge
from burning a bridge
from a leap of faith
why not now
why let it
fizzle
...?

Extreme unction

before he died all gaunt and drawn,
shrunken, skeletal, rotten teeth, hair shorn,
his eyes set, black, sucked in

the light remaining
he looked like nothing

so much as an inmate of the asylum at Charenton
his madness was exemplary
you couldn't touch it
or get anywhere near it

three-three-three-three…
he'd chunter
and look askance in anxious response
to any reach, any question, any tone
three-three-three-three-three
his fingers fidgeting, frantic or forlorn.
only song would calm him, anoint him
his eyes, his ears, his nose, his fingers, his lips
and, like the priest's thumb, carry him
over the rainbow.

Ambulo ergo sum

   thanks to Bruce Baugh for the title

I'm out walking in the wind which sings
through the rigging in the marina
and whips around citadel corner scooping up
gulls and litter as I approach the Hoe and I'm thinking
about the mind/body problem, which,
you will recall, was first delineated by Descartes
as a problem of interaction between two different
kinds of things, the one insubstantial and ghost-like
the other all shit and piss and flesh and blood,
which is of course no sort of problem at all
for most of us, and in truth, I'm thinking
of my mind/my body problem,
that part of my body called the lower digestive tract,
specifically,
that part known as the large intestine or colon
which for me, after a lifetime of giving it no regard whatsoever
has become a big problem and plays daily
on my mind and occupies my thoughts
well, at least it's not cancer, my mate says
and he had proctitis himself 25 years since
in Australia, he says, and so completely misses
the point of my preoccupation
that I can't believe I'm hearing what I'm hearing
and then my other mate pipes up, says he pissed himself
on the way home from the pub the other night
and needs to book himself a prostrate examination —

prostate, you mean, I say wearily —

as though that had some sort of relevance
and someone else says, I know what you mean, man,
and tells me their dad suffered
all his life with his bowels and he himself
has IBS, but I haven't got IBS, I say, that's
just excessive flatulence —
tell me about it, he laughs —
and not like this daily shedding of blood and mucous, I say,

and someone else suggests pads
like I hadn't thought of these things before
and I'm working up a right steam in my head
thinking all these thoughts and arguing
with all these voices who are to be fair
empathising but at the same time
trying to deflect from
the fear that rises within them
and who are to my mind
diminishing my condition while looking
through me and staring direct into the colour and shape
of their own demise and how that might feel
and, like this dog now emerging from the sea,
trying to shake off the thought of it,
bury it

and I carry on walking. There's a front coming in
over the Sound, clouds are gathering and likely
it will rain and I'll get wet and go home, dry off,
throw something in the oven, turn on the TV,
carry on

Essential remains

it is the eye, said Emerson, makes the horizon
and we slide each towards our own
trawling particularities, stories, effects
wakes merging in the solidity of the sea
as viewed from the deck of a ship
the incoherence of dreams shatters
any illusions of singularity
we might hold about ourselves
as night pours into day into night
so, we roll, magnum miraculum
we roll
the world on our back
we roll
like Atlas astride
with our sacks we roll
but I, weak-thin, clothes hanging off
I feel the cold these days
it's close and closing
I move on, light-headed, my legs heavy
a breeze sways me, fearful
at the harbour edge, a blue hand
beckons from the water
and I wonder, now that we're all GIs
discharged, streamed, hived, homogenised,
I wonder
who or what awaits at the end
of all this not-knowing
it's why we resist even as we roll
never knowing how others see us
hidden from them as we are hidden
from ourselves
and out of the depths of our disbelieving
out of our mistrust, we cry, our psalms fall
on ears inattentive to our supplication
still, we roll, and people, most people,
most of the time, talk shit
it's what language is for

there's nothing to be gained by any of this yet we roll
I make the effort and wonder
as a solitary crow flaps past, I wonder as I roll
if it is worth it, if there's a pay-off
knuckles cracking
like a reminder
like a past picked up
like a ball to run with
like all the things we've forgotten
like a promise not kept
like an idea you once had
like the diesel fumes scorching our throats as we roll
I'm over it, son, I'm over the wind, all over
these words
why use them at all when an emoji will do
there's nothing, nothing more, all of this
is all we have and we roll
we feel our way through in the dark
and rope in others in to amuse, or abuse
this we call choice, or need, or hope
we roll, blown hither and thither
we make of it what we can
we have all the time in the world
Louis sang, and not so long ago
but that's little enough and, foreshortened
as we grow, we get used to floating
as time's gravity drags us down
like a sky, sucks us under
like a patient etherised
like a modernist poem
like lame dogs we stumble and fall and rise
to fall and stumble and rise again
like an argument over dinner
like a door slammed shut
like an exit reversed
like a strategy for becoming
other
like a name, like a birth, like a word to the wise
like sobs blubbering off the tongue
fomenting grief,
like ice

like the trough of a wave
like forgiveness
like an assault —
if you look, if you pay attention, you can hear
the dead amongst us calling
like mothers for their children, calling
for the reasons for doing the things we do
they are calling
in order to find a way out of all this
find a way back to who, or what
we used to be, that old self
that less ugly, less compromised
less vindictive version
of what essentially remains hidden
we now know
remains lost.

In the garden

Woke up this morning wondering if it's worth it
rolled over and fell back to sleep.
maybe we can put it all to bed now,
do something different instead
as I could have done things differently,
marked out a different pattern with less hubris,
but then, I was always uncomfortable
with the idea of property, found it hard
to hang onto. makes me smile now,
but for years, in the precariat, walking
around with holes in my shoes, frittering
not-so-hard-earned on fripperies and drink,
well, I tell ya, it wasn't easy, but hey, we had a time,
didn't we have a time?
and it's not like you can stop it anytime soon
nights drawing in, season of mists and mellow et cetera
weird, when you stop and think about it,
that we should spend so much time on the dead,
thinking about them, owning them, these
competing narratives, these myths, these lies
struggling for ascendancy: what do we do about that?
what goes around, as they say...
even here in Sainsbury's, as the doors
slide open, like an oven's to consume me,
Adele sings, she offers to make me happy,
make my dreams come true, the thought of which
sends me scurrying off to bananas and soft fruit —
can't eat apples since the radiation
ruined my saliva glands.

His life

he used to be a Telegram boy.
14, already out of school, working.
his peak cap and uniform, dark blue, red cording
dashing round the streets on his bicycle:
these urgent messages,
births, marriages, sickness, deaths.
long gone those long days.

he whistled as he worked, sang as he worked,
loved to work
always happy as the lark in the sky as he worked
always singing,
work gave him a reason
"Telegram, Mrs…"
sometimes a penny for good news,
sometimes only tears.
"Any reply?"

a life already slipping away from him,
pulling him asunder,
the rug from under his feet
never since so securely fixed,
but always a smile, a laugh, a song.

back home, he would reach
into the larder for a pint of milk,
press down the foil with his thumb,
slip it off, guzzle it
down in one
wipe his mouth with his sleeve
Ah, he'd exhale

and you see him now, as he is,
drooling in his armchair, bound in continence pads.
his memory stuttering and fading,
the years ploughed into his face.
this is my life, he said,
looking around the demented armchair-fillers
in the lounge pooling their stares

into the vacancy at the centre of the room:
this is my life.

I knew then he was alive —
in himself, I mean —
still working on it, still there staring
into a future shrivelling into the paisley
swirls on the carpet of the care home,

still there, yet away
with his scattered thoughts, his history,
he was trying, as I too try,
as we all try,
to convince ourselves
it's not over
I am here

End of life care

good morning, make that your last cigarette.

it is the business
of the future
to be dangerous,
so said Whitehead.

can you remember any of that stuff?

the cold wind moans
slamming the door behind us
let us recall
how close we were.

whatever I touch
you touch
when I move
you move with me.

the light that was there
the original light
is still there.
dying wasn't always like this

walking backwards into the future
the present becomes me
the screen on which
the past is projected.

surrounded by possibilities
drowning in procedure
it can feel
whatever you choose
is the wrong choice

too late now
to never again
make the same mistakes.

My dying breath

first light and I awake wheezing
get up for a piss and reach
for my inhaler on the shelf

in so doing I knock
my toothbrush into the bowl
reach down to get it
when I am seized

by a dizzy
violence so sudden
it throws me back
towards the shower, in a stroke
I grab a rail to save the fall

my head balloons
in my hands
anaesthetised
I can't feel it.

now I'm shaking
like Johnny Kidd
all over all over
now
it's all over

I
Love
You.

My life and other things that never happened

things are fading, I'm thinking about
the correct way of walking,
shoulders back,
head raised staring dead
into the bright light
of a clear blue day
it's the only way
to say it,
can you see the RED BUTTON
mad
the way the city stutters
like an ox drunk on Apollinaire
or the way
the lanced shank of a bull in Las Ventas
spatters
Lorca's dancers in a red whirl
it's like a painting
it's like nothing you've ever seen before,
like a painting
like a great crowd hungry
for love, for love,
it's like a painting
it's like nothing you've ever seen,
nothing you've ever heard is like this
cumulous floats, a yellow sun
down, nothing moves
save for the dance of gnats
were it not
for the ringing in my ears,
the late light laughter of the waves,
the flap of a wing,
this could be you
this could be me
this could
be here now.

Fader

the light is fallen from the sky
the earth is spent.
my window faces north
your voice on the wind

the north wind
rattling the mail-flap in the door.
there are things to be done
you are not here.

On reading Robert Herrick with the benefit of hindsight

the way I look at things it's easy
seems like everything is fucked-up
it's all fucked-up
so fucked-up there're people going round
cooking-up realities for themselves
their world, their truth
and there's no consensus, no agreement
on anything anymore and everyone
part of some bogus community
of one sort or another
all of it in their heads
yet the world is as it's always been
cold and cruel and unfeeling
ripped apart by Freud, Jung and Wilhelm Reich
and their squalid little notions
about what things are like
it's all just more fucking metaphor
lies we tell ourselves when the world
draws too close
and I'm thinking about
all the fucking time
I've had to do
all the fucking things
I've wanted to do and how
all the fucking time
has now
run
out

Reading Peter Reading on the bus to the hospital

   for Steve Spence

travelling alone between here and there,
always here, wherever I am it is
always here always alone
never get there
never arrive never return
from here
it can't be done

je ne voudrais pas
etre mort
at moments like this in
C
I laugh out loud
know exactly what it means

Reading Rilke on the bus to the hospital

I own nothing and soon enough
will own less
my dream was always
to disappear one day
to be no-one visible to no one

I have been known to rise
and turn and walk away and keep on
walking away in a silence invisible
a no-one,
a no-thing,
a shrinking dot marking the horizon,
stuttering into darkness

Reading John Berryman on the bus to the hospital

on a blue day
I am dreaming
of a green day
of you lost now
your words ringing
drunk in your wake
we're drunk, we've been drinking
you and I, you were late,
me soon-to-be, I ask you,
I need to know,
that ball you ran to the river, to me
those tears that filled the pool
of subsequent years, the long afternoons
on barstools staring down the bubbles
rising from the bottom of your glass — did it,
did they, expand the epistemology
of your loss and help on that final
mad drive to the bridge?

If you are reading this, I am alive

the hospital calls: it wishes to read
my entrails by way of a camera
inserted in my anus
quite why they wish to do this
I'm not sure: I get conflicting views
I've been a patient so long now,
given my body up, surrendered so often to
medical opinion, manipulation and advice,
I no longer feel in control
of the flesh
I haul out like a sack of waste to be
pecked, prodded and poked by gulls
I do as I am told
and await collection
I am patient
a cool observer of procedures
performed by coolly efficient men and women
I watch on monitors as they thread
a stent through a vein in my wrist all the way
to my malfunctioning heart,
and breathe immediately
easier as they inflate the tiny balloon
to expand the stent and open the artery
I meditate on life's brief candle
and what it all means as they zap
the circumference of my neck with daily
doses of radiation to obliterate
the cancerous enemy within —
funny how one slips into sentimentalising
the fight to beat this, you can do it
my friends say and I want to believe them
but know it is all bollocks. And here
lying on my left side, knees angled
like a foetus, the Vaseline cold
I think of Marlon Brando
about to do anal reaching
behind him for butter in Last Tango
in Paris, ever the romantic, I watch

on the screen as the camera snakes
through my colon burning off and collecting
polyps, like malignant nipples on a milk-heavy
breast, and think of many reasons to call a halt
to the procedure, put an end to it.
yet, when the implement is withdrawn and
the consultant asks if I've had my prostate
checked recently and suggests I should:
I'll put it in the report, he says.
I shrug and sigh and say,
yeah, fine, ok, thanks. and go
and get dressed and on the bus home
make notes and wonder if this
is a suitable subject for poetry.

The old place

back again, the old place changed
in truth, hardly at all
they gather, hungry for you,
for a piece of you, around the door
that same emptiness fills your thought

and it's fear keeps you here
keeps you coming back
fear of the thought itself
out there with a wild love
out there in the cold
with a wild love
and you exposed
running naked mad
down Robinswood and Crossacres
your hair all a-shiver
with a wild love
a wild love dancing all around you
love

you recall
how sticky was the sap bleeding
from the pines,
the long hours at the side of the road
bewildered by traffic and diesel fumes
heat rising from the tarmac
and you turn back too late,
too late turn back
because it's always too late.

and these clouds drifting across
an almost sky
contribute almost nothing
to these almost days
clouds which are in truth

ghosts formed of old newspaper sheets
left behind to line drawers

whereas you, you learned
to fake it out there
with a cock-eyed smile
a punch or a monkey wrench
angled just so
to deliver gifts
of poppy seeds and tart fruit
platitudes hanging off you
like cheap clothes
musty, moth-eaten,

falling apart
you read the news
men have walked on the moon
Meredith Hunter's blood's still warm
The Beatles have broken up
and a future like gravity
hauls you in the drumbeat of
its time signature
cuts crotchets and quavers
in your skin
hauls you in
your skin, desiccated,
curls yellow
like ancient parchment
found in a desert
runes read by strangers

so

and

that's the way it is

one day's much like another
your skin's music has an irregular pulse
out of time
like a limp you carry
down the long years where nothing moves

except the sands
and the slow imperceptible
slide of your skin
and you return
to the place you were
before the place you were before
you no longer feel the weather
and carry great, ominous silences within
leviathans gliding through discord.

Listen

there will be no happiness for you,
the hen won't lay and the cock won't crow
come, come listen,
to the beating of our blood
our mighty blood pitched so low
there will be no happiness for us
our fathers will fall
and rain will fall
and disdain will be our mothers' prayer
and heavy fruit rotting on the vine
will haul down the law
tall trees will rise
spreading roots cause the pavements to crack
crumble and buildings to fall
St Pauls to fall
Westminster to fall
great cities to fall
London, Beijing, Moscow, New York all fall
the mouths of the subway stations agape
the light alone closing
for the love of God
for all mankind.

those clouds, are they seed
or are they dust?

All hope

adding
the sum
of all
my parts
the things
I do
things to
forget
now we
are who
we are
and then
we are
no more
no one

comes to
nothing

Voices on a great sea rising and falling

the swell and slip of it all
from singularities shattered
to submergence in dreams

what we make of it
we secrete in song

la mer, qu'on voit danser
night and day
you are the one
as nothing
is to I
as everything
is to me
I lie

awake and listen
to the heavy night
breathing
compassion
for the brutes
the tyrants
the fools.

Demise

gums shrunk to tissue
his teeth were rotten and falling out
they tried to x-ray
but he was afraid of the machine and shied away
like a horse
the decision was taken to remove most of them
and he spent what time he had left
with an asylum gurn and lurch,
eating slop with a spoon in his fist.

How it happened

why he was there
he was unable to say
crashing across the moor
forgetful, full of forget
his clothes sodden
the vast intemperate nothingness
of it all worn like a shroud.
his skin paper-thin,
veins pulsing beneath
blue neon flashes over the ruins
where a lewd moon rose bulbous

futile now to plunge into the pool
nothing lives there since they
drained it last Fall
fish flapping in the mud
suck air, suck sewage.

Post mortem

in the days after you died
the streets filled with relative strangers
who crossed over to avoid their eyes
meeting mine.

in the weeks after you died
traffic began to move again
and colour returned pale at first
translucent.

in the months after you died
conversation turned to other affairs
anniversaries to attend to and yours
fast approaching.

in the years after you died
rarely spoken of you were never
far away your infusions dilated
under glass.

a generation after you died
all that remains after memory
a gesture in a child or a smile
is guilt.

Squamous cell carcinoma

It grows
It eats my flesh
It grows
It consumes my thought
It grows
this thing
It grows
i sing my body
alive
It grows
It sucks me in
side out so i am stranger
to myself
than this stranger
Itself: still
It grows
this thing inside
this thing
It grows, It spreads, It burns
It stings
It riddles my memories
like so many stones
slivers of bone
fossils of greed
anger, want, fear and need
this thing
It grows these things
and grows

Elephant

he was always a funny bugger.
ach that's just his way, said our mum
kept things tight
minimal
schtum.

bedraggled fool
what world gave rise to this cretinous hulk?
did he know he was rumbled? did he still have hopes
when the needles were out, the restraints and the ropes?

grumbling, brooding
he'd shuffle his stupendous bulk
through shambolic forests of gloom,
crunching through biscuit after biscuit after biscuit
a trail of crumbs spread across the living room
nothing remembered, not day, not night
some old army buddies
some old sentimental song
awkward in captivity
uprooting chairs he'd trample
up and down the stairs
slow rising rogue anger
turned
in his slow lumbering, gait.

friends began to drift
leave him out in the cold
no more invites to golf
no longer in on the joke
he's lost, they said,

his sense of humour
befuddled when he bought them
Christmas gifts in October.
the same M&S napkins
two or three times over.

it was embarrassing,
but nobody picked up what
exactly was fruiting inside
that vast cornucopia of puzzles and knots.

he's changed,
they said, he's not
the man he used to be
they didn't twig. neither did he.

even after that incident last year
when he left a few grand,
his winnings from a nag,
in the pub, in a Tesco bag.

then, in the Indian after a session
when he shat himself
they had to lay newspaper on the seat
and taxi him home in their hurry
to wash their hands
and return to their curry

only then
did they know. How could they before?
there was no outward sign
his breathing was fine
he didn't clutch his chest,
stagger, didn't have a fall.
it wasn't that kind of thing at all.

they just thought him odd
and were right, but afraid to allow
the noise of reason gone wrong
they didn't seek him out
after all
you can't wring tears
from irrational fears.

but the notes he made to remind himself
pathetically printed in wavering hand
in that little book he always forgot:

cards in top drawer, hat on stand, keys in bowl
that kind of thing, told their own

story if only he could have read it
instead, he followed obsessive habit
morning coffee, bread, butter and jam
drive to the station at 8.30 a.m.
that regular pulse he thought kept him on track
and it did, at least
on the days when he found his way back.

until that day
the doctor at the memory clinic said,
the lesions you see here and here and
these patches here,
they are causing this
and you must now stop driving:
it's illegal for you to drive your self
now that I have told you this.

knocked back
stunned stupid.
stopped in his tracks.
infantilised, he didn't see
how could he?
or understand what was said
but knew somehow the game was up
that he couldn't with
the pretence grappling in the wrong order
continue could he with words
that it was it wasn't was — what?
happening
and to him
what was left of him

and so he heaved, lay down his mass
put aside his carapace
as rips and tears
ruined his great face

There is a sickness at the heart of this

it was a bright yellow raincoat falling
not quite a raincoat, more an idea of time
time as a raincoat falling, a yellow raincoat
falling and rising like a monstrous bird on thermals:
they thought it would be easy to find in the search
but they missed a trick and took the wrong road
everywhere there is music and music in time
it can't be stopped. what was it Chekhov said?
people live their most interesting lives as a secret
and according to Camus the only true philosophical
problem is suicide. are we destined then to fail
to fall carried by currents? what can we do
about ourselves asking the same questions
over and over? we have no deep sense yet
of the horror of it all, the way he looked at her
it was crazy-making she said and he put his head
on my lap and began sobbing,
you're offering me roses
she said, what is this?
he was uncanny
with his physical connection to all around him
alert, like an animal in his responses to it
and there is a sickness at the heart of this.
she smiled all the time and was very inquisitive
until she saw him naked under the blanket
that time, smiling at her.
it was a trick, he said, all part of the game, he said
and it didn't take long before the interstates
morphed into a nightmare logistics
facilitating the smooth transport of transgressions
and our fairytale world stopped
and all roads led back to Seattle.

what should we do with unwanted information?
what are we here for?
what are we doing with our lives?

Song of living too long

falling, falling, falling through
each night, the way it is, and each room delirious with youth
and drunk on fiddle, guitar and mandolin
and mouths open wide as the long future and lusty with song
sang of love and loss and hope for the long future
and the streets drunk on music, on the way it is, it was
glorious, glorious and sadder than Christmas, normal stuff
and it's not being old in itself, but living too long
that's the problem. Yes, it's living too long through
the way it is, the way we are, the way we do things,
the habits, expectations, the way we fall and rise to fall
again that's the problem, the weariness with it all
as sleep comes over us, or is denied us and we sink again
into pattern again, the old things again, the old songs
searching there for clues or reasons for the way we are
the way we do the things we do, the roles we assume
the way it is when you strip it all back or add it all up
and whether you do one or the other, makes no difference
you still do them, they are done. It's the way it is.
fortune favours the brave and all the old baloney,
stuff you get told, stuff you pick up, stuff you make up,
fuck up, makes all the difference to the person you are,
yet, you are that person that does the things you do
the way you do them, the way it is. Like that time
before everything got out of hand, before the need
to understand, before the need for lies, the need
to open a conversation with myself, when there was peace
in my heart, before I capitulated, when I could point
like a child, point and say, there, there, Daddy, let's go
there, let's see! and we'd go, drop everything and go.
when we were out of control,
before the masks and the roles
didn't think too much about the whos the whats the whys
the clothes we wore, when everything was different,
that it was ugly and insidious didn't matter,
was hidden from us,
we didn't care, cared only that we'd found each other,
not that we were right or wrong, there was no future
then, no past. never really got over that.

In the dark, I feel my eye turn and play. he didn't like me,
the way he looked at me, the disdain, suspicion,
though we never spoke, it was all eyes and I feel my eye turn
in the dark and play and wonder what he thinks, standing there,
looking out to sea, the wide-open sea and the wide cloudy sky,
running through all the questions in his head, my head,
all the questions running through my head, the tropes
we build for ourselves, the traps
we fall into, Icarus falling,
Daedalus, twiddling thumbs, watching his son falling,
falling as the sun rises, falling,
past the mountains
past the books, the mountains of books
falling past the fly-tips,
the junk, the waste, the years,
the gulls and the clowns
and the twin tongues of flame
ghosting us
in the dark,
I feel my eye
turn in the dark
play in the dark
the dark dark dark

Deadlines

1.

the help I'll need
with my demise
a tab of acid
a house with windows
a view of the sky

2.

beached
shale slipping
grip failing
tide incoming
shush there shush
darkness
stones
washed away

3.

something
words that are not words
truths that are not truths
something
about something
some guiding principle
something attempting
to be said
something emerging
through walls
from another room
sounds
like voices
whispers

4.

light out
like a star burning
go up there
sit
one last stroke
a hand, a pen
going down
that fat red sun
going down

5.

telos
the totality of things
what is
yet could not be
or be other
than what it is

Thinking about it

I think about it more these days
I think about it most days
crossing the street, I think about it
quicken my step and think about it
breathe easier on reaching the other side
I come home, cook some food and
think about it
what I'm doing about it
I go to bed thinking about it
I wake up in the night for a piss and think about it
I'm thinking about it now
writing this, I'm thinking about it
this is about it
about me thinking about it
it follows me around
like a faithful old dog at my heel
I can't help but think about it
can't ignore it, can't shoo it away, can't have it put down
I don't want to, but can't stop thinking about it
it's dogged, it persists, insists,
when I'm not thinking about it, I know
I'll be thinking about it soon enough
swallowing my meds reminds me, as if I need reminding,
to think about it and thinking about it
I can't think what I'll miss
when I think no more
about it.

Absence

and what she wrote to him
that day, years later
and years out of his innocence,
how she saw the swallows return
and thought of absence then,
of absence and the mysterious flow of things
one into the other
and all the things we can never know,
never get purchase on,
that only faith can hold to scrutiny
and if we lose it, we are lost,
lost ones
no longer at one with ourselves,
no longer capable of making sense
of the insensible,
of opinion,
so imbued with facticity,
amorphous,
like clay thrown on a wheel,
like futures indistinguishable
from memory.

I've grown old

the imprint of your dna sequence code
ticking still in my blood, I carry your breath
cold, cupped in my hands
north
and maybe there,
far away from the traffic
and the frantic business
of doing, maybe there
where the snowy owl sweeps
low over the tundra at dusk
without a sound and the white wind
wails with the wolf down the trails
of the bears and the dead
and the white-
out everywhere alone
and slow as the sky
bruises, maybe there
one blue star
inhales.

Redshift

I was young then — or old, as they saw me —
riding the long slow train
on the ancient route across the Gobi,
heading west.
The Great Wall of rammed earth
ran alongside the track —
here, the relic of five dynasties:
the Warring States, Qin, Han, Northern Liang, and Ming.
I was chain-smoking with my three companions,
drinking green tea, sharing fruit, cigarettes and seeds,
spitting pips on the floor
of the soft-sleeper compartment,
and staring out the window, trying
to comprehend the distance from 475 BCE to 1346 CE —
the years rolling past in red earth,
rammed with ancient red willow, reeds and bone,
bone-dry now, crumbling in the dry red heat.
vast tracts of time and time's reasons framed by the window,
and the long green slow train rocking through it all,
through time's flow, and I gentle rocking
with the train from side to side,
to side to side,
to side...

It was a little after dawn.
I'd come 6,000 miles from my roots,
abandoned by my ghosts, I could see
the world pellucid now, shining through.
Outside me now, all I'd forgotten made me:
my lonely childhood, my angry youth kicking back,
the years of drunkenness and fervour —
my children forgive me, for I was bereft —
and now divested of fear,
of hope, law, language, idea,
now I knew nothing —
was out, out, away and clear,
and the great future coming
soft as a fist through fog.

I dreamt a poem, and a kindness came upon me,
enveloped my innocence like an idea of nothing —
like an idea of God.

The great cities falling behind me now:
Babel, Babylon to Beijing, from Xanadu to Xian;
and all through the straits of insomnia, the dream stupas,
prayer-wheels of the eternal, sky burials,
citadels and minarets, pagodas,
swooping temple roofs — Daoist, Confucian, Buddhist —
onion domes, spires, obelisks,
skyscrapers of wonder, the money, the fear;
and the railway stations crushed-crazy,
chaotic, cantankerous with passengers
and pickpockets and traders hawking
ganmian, roujiamo, baozi,
yangrou chuan, ji jiao, bing tanghulu;
and the impossible luggage — buckets, sacks, boxes —
and birds crashing against the windows,
the money and the fear, and the memory
of the lost ones in rags, in boats adrift and sinking
and the shibboleths forking over the delta plains of history
to deposit sword and gun, pen and proclamation,
cyber-hacks and division in the silt —
all was behind me, all was lost,
all was love, all was weeping,
all was love,
like a million Christs in despair and wonder in Gethsemane,
crying out, not here, not here, my God, not here!
And the very earth was love and red with blood,
and stillness burned in the slow red-shift
of the desert in my eyes,
the sun now up and bleeding shadows.
My companions awake, oblivious —
they share filthy stories, they smoke,
they cackle, they hawk and spit on the floor...

And it all comes back to me — or I to it —
on this long slow train rolling over
expansion gaps, through Euclidean spaces of desire and dream,
the warped topology of our manifold histories
of what we forget remembers us:
what we were
what we are
what becomes us.

Photo credit: Si Hackers

Brian Herdman is a caucasian male, but not yet dead. Rumours to the contrary are false — at the time of writing.

ALSO BY BRIAN HERDMAN

78 45 33

www.ingramcontent.com/pod-product-compliance
Lightning Source LLC
Chambersburg PA
CBHW032229080426
42735CB00008B/781